HAIR STYLIST

© 2024 Julie Dascoli

All rights reserved. No part of this book may be reproduced or transmitted in any form or by any means, electronic or mechanical, including photocopying, recording or by any information storage and retrieval system, without prior permission in writing from the publisher.

Published in 2024 by Amba Press, Melbourne, Australia.
www.ambapress.com.au

Previously published in 2015 by Hawker Brownlow Education.
This edition replaces all previous editions.

ISBN: 9781923116825 (pbk)
ISBN: 9781923116832 (ebk)

A catalogue record for this book is available from the National Library of Australia.

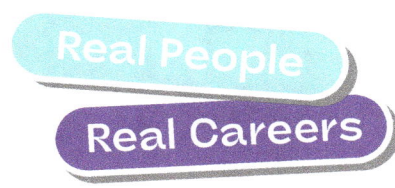

HAIR STYLIST

Written by Julie Dascoli

Photography by Laura Dascoli

Dear Reader,

Welcome to this volume of the *Real People Real Careers* series. I hope you'll enjoy learning about another exciting job people can do.

Before you read on, I'd like to say a few thank-yous to the people who helped to make this book possible.

Firstly, thank you to Laura Dascoli, who took the photographs you see in the book, and to Donna Dascoli, who provided initial editing and computer support services.

Secondly, my thanks to the staff and students in Years 4, 5 and 6 of the Mossgiel Park Primary School class of 2016 for their unwavering help and support.

And finally, I'm doubly grateful to Lisa, who generously gave up her time to help others learn about her profession — and to show them all the ways in which her job rules!

Happy reading!

Julie Dascoli

HAIR STYLIST

My name is Lisa, and I am a **hair stylist** and hairdresser.

In year ten, I did **work experience** like a lot of students do. Work experience gives a student an opportunity to sample a chosen job for a short amount of time without commitment from the student or the **employer**.

I enjoyed my work experience so much, and was **elated** when the **Salon** offered me an **apprenticeship**. I couldn't wait to start. I began working with the manager and two other qualified Hairdressers. It was great to have three people to learn from, as everyone has their own way of doing things.

After a three-month **probation period**, my **employer** enrolled me in **TAFE** which I attended one day per week. At TAFE I studied for a Certificate III in Hairdressing which included subjects like science and business.

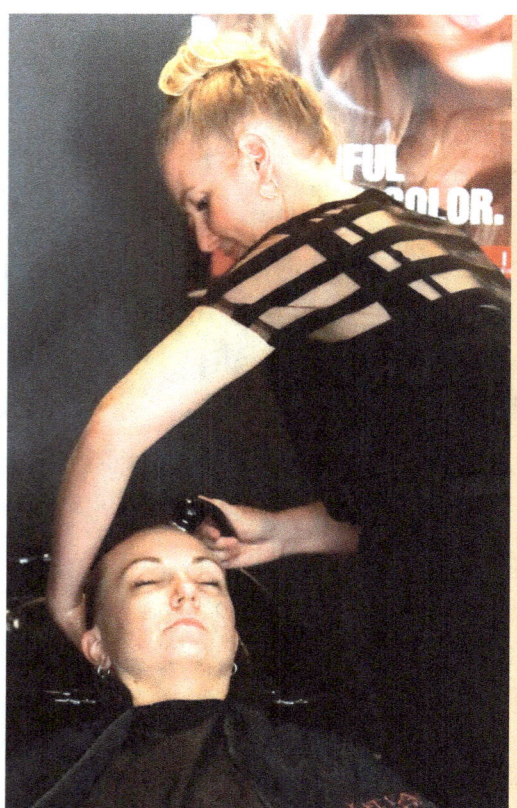

It was great to have three people to learn from, as everyone has their own way of doing things.

In the salon I started off doing tasks like sweeping the floors, cleaning the benches and changing the **sterilisers**. Next I learned how to wash people's hair and answer the phone. I learned how to talk to the **clients** by observing the other staff and imitating them.

I worked really hard, and was very quickly encouraged to start working on client's hair. I started with **blow-waves**, **setting in rollers** and simple haircuts.

TAFE was also going really well and I was able to, with a lot of hard work, finish the three-year course in just eighteen months. This is called a **self-paced course**. The duration of the apprenticeship was still four years, but I no longer had to go to TAFE and was only working in the salon.

I now started to develop my own **clientele**. In addition to working in the salon, my employer sent me to extra training courses whenever they were available.

In my final year I was nominated for the Apprentice of the Year award. I did not win but I was proud to be nominated.

This was the time I decided to **advance** myself. When I saw an advertisement for a qualified hairdresser in a prominent city salon I applied and got the job. This was an amazing experience. At this salon we did the hair of many famous celebrities for many events such as the **Logies** and the **Brownlow medal ceremony**.

I enjoyed working there so much and learnt a lot, but eventually it became too difficult to travel to the city. With the traffic, the cost of parking and the very long hours beginning to take their toll, it was back to the suburbs for me.

My next job was with a **manager** that was not very nice to work for. After great working experiences in the past this made me very unhappy. My choices were to put up with it, find another job or buy a salon of my own and work for myself.

I looked at a few salons for sale, and after borrowing money from the bank I finally settled for one. This was very scary, but super exciting at the same time.

I took over the salon and **hired** two qualified Hairdressers and an apprentice to work with me. I was off and running. The salon became busier and busier. It was fantastic. The girls I had working for me were terrific and I was able to leave them in charge and do some courses in spray-tanning, nail technology, waxing and make-up application. The salon now offered a full range of hair and beauty services.

Applying hair tint

It took me a few years to complete these courses, as I also got married and had my three children in the meantime. My apprentice is now qualified, and I only need to go back to work for three days per week so I can both service my clients and care for my family.

I love my work; creating styles and seeing clients leave with smiles is immensely rewarding. But equally important is being there for my children, helping with homework and sharing bedtime stories. It's a dance of snipping and styling at the salon, then switching to hugs and family dinners at home.

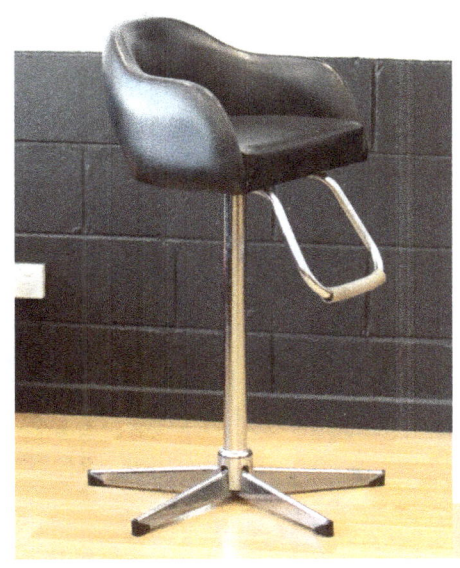
Children's high chair

Customer waiting area

HAIR STYLIST

Some of the tasks I perform every day are:

- → dropping the children off at school, kinder or daycare
- → unlocking the shop, and starting up the heater or air-conditioner (depending on the weather)
- → checking the appointment book, and preparing equipment for the first few appointments
- → greeting staff and discussing the day to come
- → beginning to greet and consult with clients as they arrive
- → placing orders for stock as required
- → packing up, cleaning up, gathering towels to take home for washing
- → setting up for the next day
- → locking up and leaving

Cash register

Interesting facts

- I have approximately 400 clients.
- My favourite task is doing hair for weddings and special occasions.
- My least favourite task is cleaning up and folding foils.
- I have approximately 30 minutes for a lunch break.
- My dream job is doing what I am doing now. However I would one day love to do high-profile work for television or celebrities again.
- The hair I cut from people's heads either goes in the rubbish bin or compost bin.
- I sometimes snip my knuckles when I'm cutting but I have never snipped a customer.
- I occasionally trim my own hair.
- I do men, women and children's hair.

Blow-wave brushes

Hair washing basin chair

Hair products

Work station

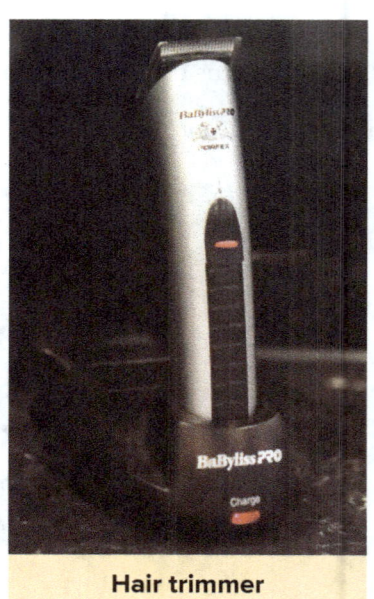
Hair trimmer

When I go to work I don't wear a specific uniform, however I only wear black clothing, just in case I spill hair tint or other products on my clothes. I also wear a protective apron when I need to do messy jobs to further protect against me ruining my clothes.

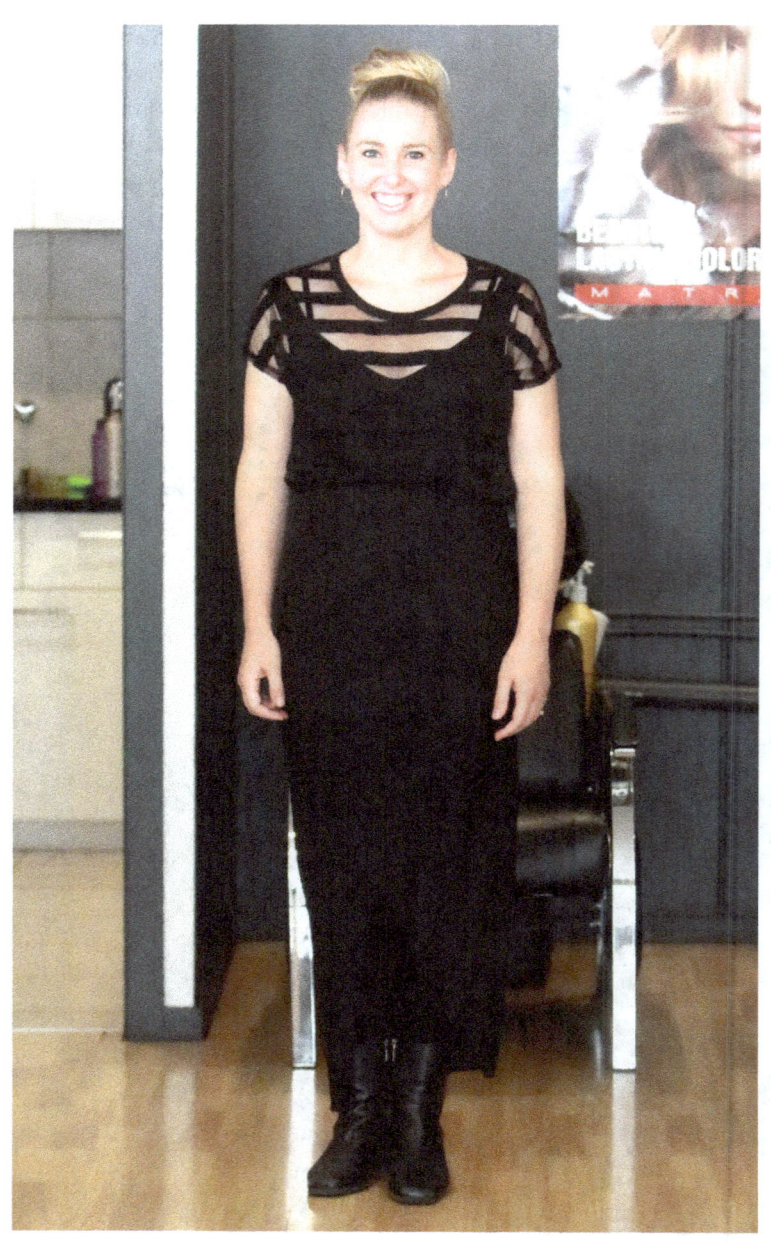

Associated occupations

- → Hairdresser's Receptionist
- → Nail Technician
- → Beauty Therapist
- → Colourist
- → Stylist
- → Barber
- → Make Up Artist

You could do my job if you:

- → enjoy working with people
- → are creative
- → have patience
- → are polite
- → are a good listener
- → show initiative

Lisa continues to juggle the difficult task of running the salon and caring for her family. The salon is going from strength to strength, with new things being added all the time to improve the business. She recently added a special room to the salon for brides and their wedding parties to prepare for their special day, and she runs children's pamper parties for special occasions.

Glossary

Advance	To move ahead or improve. *Lisa soon knew when it was time to advance herself.*
Apprenticeship	A type of training that combines hands on, on the job work with TAFE studies for a period of three or four years. After this time, the Apprentice will be a qualified tradesperson. *Lisa obtained her hairdressing qualification by doing an apprenticeship for four years.*
Blow-waves	Creating a hairstyle using hot air from a hairdryer and shaping with a brush. *One of the first things Lisa learned to do to client's hair was a blow-wave.*
Brownlow medal ceremony	An award ceremony to celebrate the best and fairest of the Australian rules football competition. *Lisa worked on the hair of those who were attending the Brownlow medal ceremony.*
Cash register	A machine that calculates and stores money in a shop. *Lisa has a cash register to help manage the money in her salon.*
Clientele	The regular customers of a particular business. Often these customers ask for a particular operator. *Clients soon started asking for Lisa to do their hair and very quickly she had her own clientele.*

Elated	Extremely happy. *Lisa was elated when she was offered a job at the salon where she was doing work experience.*
Employer	A person who provides a job for someone. *An employer gave Lisa a chance to experience Hairdressing.*
Hired	To agree to give someone a job in exchange for wages. *Lisa hired some staff to help her operate her new salon.*
Logies	An award ceremony celebrating the achievements of the Australian television industry. *Lisa worked on the hair of those who were attending the Logies.*
Manager	A person employed to run a business when the owner is not there. *Lisa worked for a manager who was not very nice to her.*
Nail technology	The study of the use of tools, equipment and other products used to treat, take care of and beautify client's nails. A Nail Technician is a person who is qualified in nail technology. *Lisa did a course to learn how to do people's fingernails.*
Nominated	To be suggested for a position, award or honour. *Lisa was nominated for apprentice of the year. This is an enormous honour.*

Probation period	A short time at the beginning of a new job where the supervisor watches over the new employee closely to make sure they meet the standards as expected. *Lisa had a three-month probation period before her employer committed to continuing her employment at the salon.*
Salon	A place where hairdressing or beauty services are provided. *The Salon offered Lisa an apprenticeship.*
Self-paced course	Taking on study that the student can work at their own pace to finish, and can potentially complete more quickly. *Lisa worked really hard in her self-paced course and was able to complete the schooling part of her apprenticeship very early.*
Setting in rollers	Creating a hairstyle by putting a series of different-sized rollers (a small barrel) in wet hair and, upon drying, combing the hair out into a style. *One of the first tasks Lisa learned to do to client's hair was to set in rollers.*
Spray-tanning	A procedure where a client can be sprayed with a solution to stain the skin and imitate a suntan. *Lisa did a course to learn how to do spray-tans.*

Steriliser	Hairdressers must sterilise their equipment in sterilisers to ensure that germs are not spread from client to client. There are dry and liquid sterilisers that need their water changed every day. *Lisa makes sure the sterilisers have the water changed every day.*
TAFE	Technical and Further Education. A vocational school where people can learn the technical skills they need to do their jobs and earn a certificate or diploma. *Lisa went to TAFE and finished her qualification early because she worked really hard.*
Waxing	The removal of unwanted hair from client's bodies. *One of the courses Lisa did was waxing.*
Work experience	A short-term placement within a business to give a student an idea of what it is like to do a particular job. *Lisa did work experience as a Hairdresser and loved it.*
Workstation	Area where the client sits to have their hair done. This includes a mirror, bench and chair. *Lisa's salon has five workstations.*

Other titles in this series

 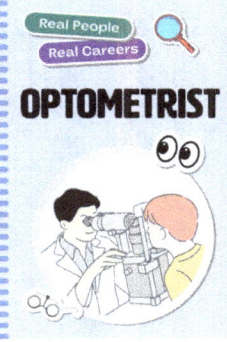 

www.ingramcontent.com/pod-product-compliance
Lightning Source LLC
Chambersburg PA
CBHW070343120526
44590CB00017B/2998